C000149059

Millfield Prep School

08937

Who were the Romans?
Qui erant Romani?

Adapted from *Who were the Romans?*
in the Usborne Starting Point History series by
Nicole Irving

Latin text by **Graham Tingay**

Original book by **Phil Roxbee Cox**

Illustrated by **Annabel Spenceley**
Designed by **Diane Thistlethwaite**

Additional illustrations by Kate Davies
With thanks to Andy Dixon and John Russell

Series editor: Jane Chisholm
History consultant: Dr Anne Millard

CONTENTS

MILLFIELD PREP SCHOOL
LIBRARY

Qui erant Romani? Who were the Romans?

Urbs Roma amplius duo milia et quingentos annos fuit. nunc caput Italiae, temporibus antiquis caput imperii ingentis erat.

The city of Rome has existed for over two and a half thousand years. Now it is the capital of Italy, but in ancient times, it was at the heart of a huge empire.

Romani erant ei qui aut Romae aut in imperio Romano habitabant. Latine loquebantur. quo tempore imperium erat maximum circiter sescentiens centena milia capitum habitantium erant.

The Romans were people who lived in Rome or the Roman Empire. They spoke Latin. When the empire was at its biggest, there were about 60 million inhabitants.

Senatores, saepe patricii, Romam gubernabant.
The senators, who were often aristocrats, governed Rome.

Plebs
Ordinary citizens

Equites negotium mercatumque suscipiebant.
The equites ran business and trade.

Qui erant cives? Who were citizens?

De Romanis alii cives, alii non cives erant. cives omnia quae volebant, si non contra leges, faciebant. viri qui cives erant etiam suffragium ferre poterant.

Some Romans were citizens, others were not. Citizens could do what they liked, so long as it was not against the law. Men who were citizens could also vote.

Qui erant servi? Who were slaves?

Servi non cives, sed proprium dominorum erant. omnia opera horribilia faciebant, et pretium vel minimum vel nullum accipiebant.

Slaves were not citizens, but belonged to their masters. They did all the horrible jobs and got little or no pay.

2

Qui Romam condiderunt? **Who founded Rome?**

Olim lupa, ut fabula Romanorum narrat, geminos infantes ad Tiberim flumen invenit. tum pastor uxorque eos educavit.

According to a Roman legend, once upon a time a she-wolf found baby twins by the River Tiber. Then a shepherd and his wife brought them up.

Postea gemini, Romulus et Remus, urbem Romam in eodem loco prope Tiberim condiderunt. Romulus, Remo occiso, Romam e suo nomine nominavit.

The twins, Romulus and Remus, later founded the city of Rome on the same spot near the Tiber. Having killed Remus, Romulus named Rome after himself.

Servi feminam divitem in sella peculiari, lectica vocata, ferunt
Slaves carrying a rich woman in a special chair, called a litter

Statura lupae
Statue of the she-wolf

Servi
Slaves

Quid est lingua Latina? **What is Latin?**

Romani Latine loquebantur. multa verba multarum linguarum e lingua Latina veniunt. verbum nostrum **language** e verbo Latino "lingua" venit.

Latin is the language the Romans spoke. Many words in many languages come from Latin. Our word "language" comes from the Latin word for "tongue".

Quis erat Julius Caesar? **Who was Julius Caesar?**

Imperator erat praeclarus, qui Romam regebat. gratiosus erat, sed ei erant inimici, qui eum occiderunt anno XLIV a.Chr.n.

He was a famous general, who ruled Rome. He was popular but had enemies, who killed him in 44BC*.

Quomodo de Romanis cognovimus? **How do we know about the Romans?**

Multa de Roma antiqua cognovimus e reliquis aedificorum eo tempore constructorum. his effossis de vita Romanorum cotidiana plura percipimus.

We know a lot about Ancient Rome from what is left of buildings built at that time. By digging them up, we understand more about the Romans' daily life.

Amphorae
Wine jars

Mensa
Bar

Hi effodiunt cauponam.
These people are digging up a wine bar.

Multa etiam a Romanis scripta supersurt, quae imaginem vitae eorum cotidianae nobis augent.

Many things written by Romans also survive, which add to our picture of their daily life.

*The Latin a.Chr.n. stands for ante Christum natum, which means "before the birth of Christ", or BC. The year 44BC was 44 years before the birth of Christ (which was at the start of year 1). For Latin numbers, see page 13.

Quae erat species Romanorum?
What did the Romans look like?

Romani primi e genere Latino orti sunt. eis erant vultus fuscus crinesque nigri. mox imperio crescente, cum aliis gentibus commixti, multos specie varia continebant.

The first Romans came from a tribe called the Latins. They had olive skin and black hair. As the empire grew, they mixed with other races and soon included lots of people with different looks.

Haec pictura in tabula est juvenis Romanae divitis.
This is a wall-painting of a wealthy young Roman woman.

Quem vestitum gerebant? What clothes did they wear?

Viri tunicam gerebant. si cives erant, vestimentum candidum, togam vocatum, super tunicam induere licebat.

Men wore a tunic. If they were citizens, they could wear a white robe, called a toga, over the tunic.

Feminae quoque tunicas gerebant. supra, stolam simplicem nitidamque induebant. vestes coloribus ex herbis vel murice extractis tingebant.

Women also wore tunics. On top, they wore a bright, simple dress. They dyed their clothes with dyes made from plants or shellfish.

Tunica
Tunic

Vestimentum simplex, stola vocatum
Simple dress, called "stola"

Stola super tunicam induta
Stola worn over a tunic

Romani speculi ex aere polito fictis utebantur.
The Romans had mirrors made from polished bronze.

Tonsoris puer
Barber's slave-assistant

Barba munde recisa
Neatly trimmed beard

Soleae Sandals

Calceamentis utebantur?
Did they have shoes?

Sane, multa et varia genera. saepe etiam soleas gerebant.

Yes, lots of different kinds. They often wore sandals, too.

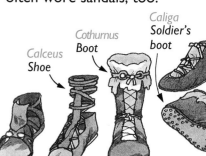

Caliga
Soldier's boot

Cothurnus
Boot

Calceus
Shoe

Toga
Toga

4

Medicamina faciei adhibebant?
Did they wear make-up?

Certe feminae. speciem habere pallidam malebant, itaque pulvere cretae utebantur. palpebras etiam cinere, labra faece tingebant. divites, et viri et feminae, odores adhibebant sumptuosos.

Yes, women did. They liked to look pale, so they used chalk powder. They also made up their eyelids with ash and their lips with wine. Well-off men and women wore expensive perfumes.

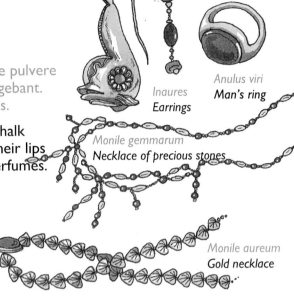

Inaures
Earrings

Anulus viri
Man's ring

Monile gemmarum
Necklace of precious stones

Monile aureum
Gold necklace

Armilla aurea
Gold bracelet

Odor
Perfume

Pecten
Comb

Qualia ornamenta erant?
What were their jewels like?

Romanae, si satis divites erant, ornamenta gerebant mirabilia, auro, ebore, gemmis confecta. et viri et feminae anulos interdumque fibulas induebant.

Roman women, if they were rich enough, wore wonderful jewels made of gold, ivory and precious stones. Both men and women wore rings and sometimes brooches.

Laurea
Headband of laurel leaves (worn by generals and poets)

Fac togam tuam   Make your own toga

Togae erant maximae. togam linteo vetere forficibus caeso facere potes.

Togas were very large. You can make one by cutting up an old sheet with scissors.

Toga pueri Romani

A Roman boy's toga

← 2.75m (9ft) →

1.10m (4ft 6in)

Impone unum togae extremum super umerum sinistrum.

Put one end of the toga over your left shoulder.

Cingulum
Belt

Affer alterum extremum sub bracchium dextrum.

Bring the other end up under your right arm.

Tunica
Tunic

Jace hoc extremum super umerum sinistrum.

Throw this end over your left shoulder.

Insere medium togae in cingulum.

Tuck the middle of the toga into your belt.

Quales erant domus?
What were houses like?

Divites saepe et domum in urbe et villam ruri possidebant. e reliquis plerique in cenaculis conductis habitabant.

Rich people owned a town house and a country house. Most other people lived in rented apartments.

Qualia erant cenacula?
What were apartments like?

Alia lauta erant, alia cellam unam solam habebant. pauperes in cenaculis habitabant, quae viliora erant. ligno constructa facile ignem comprehendebant.

Some were luxurious, others had only one room. Poor people lived in upper-floor apartments, which were cheaper. They were built of wood and easily caught fire.

Insula
A Roman apartment building

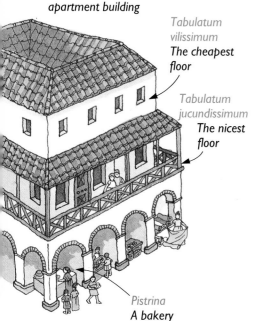

Tabulatum vilissimum
The cheapest floor

Tabulatum jucundissimum
The nicest floor

Pistrina
A bakery

Villa
A country house

Hortus
Garden

Qualia erant interiora domus?
What was the inside of a town house like?

Pictura a dextra parte speciem domus Romani divitis patefacit.

The picture on the right shows you what the house of a wealthy Roman looked like.

A. *Atrium*
Main meeting room

B. *Tablinum patrisfamilias*
The master's study

C. *Impluvium*
Pool for catching rainwater

D. *Triclinium*
Dining room

E. *Ala*
Side room

F. *Taberna*
Room rented out as a shop or store

G. *Culina*
Kitchen

H. *Cubicula*
Bedrooms

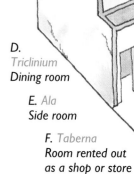

Quomodo parietes exornabant?
How did they decorate the walls?

Saepe picturas in parietibus pingebant. hae tabulae imaginem rusticam describunt.

They often painted pictures on the walls. These pictures show a countryside scene.

Lumina-ne habebant?
Did they have lights?

Ita vero, genera lucernarum varia erant. oleum ex oleis, nucibus, seminibus, piscibus expressum urebant.

Yes, there were different types of lamp. They burned oil pressed from olives, nuts, seeds or fish.

Filum
Wick

Lucerna fictilis
Pottery lamp

Lanterna pensilis e vitro et aere ficta
Hanging lantern made of glass and bronze

Candelabrum
Lamp-stand

Pictura tessellata
Mosaic picture

Qualia sola erant?
What were floors like?

Pleraque sola lapide vel terra constrata erant. in domibus lautis pavimenta tesselata erant. haec calculis variis facta erant. hi calculi, in calcem harenatum umidumque impressi, sic formas geometricas vel picturas fingebant.

Most floors were made of stone or earth. In elegant houses, there were mosaic floors. These were made from small pieces of different kinds of stone. These small pieces of stone were pressed into wet plaster and formed patterns or pictures.

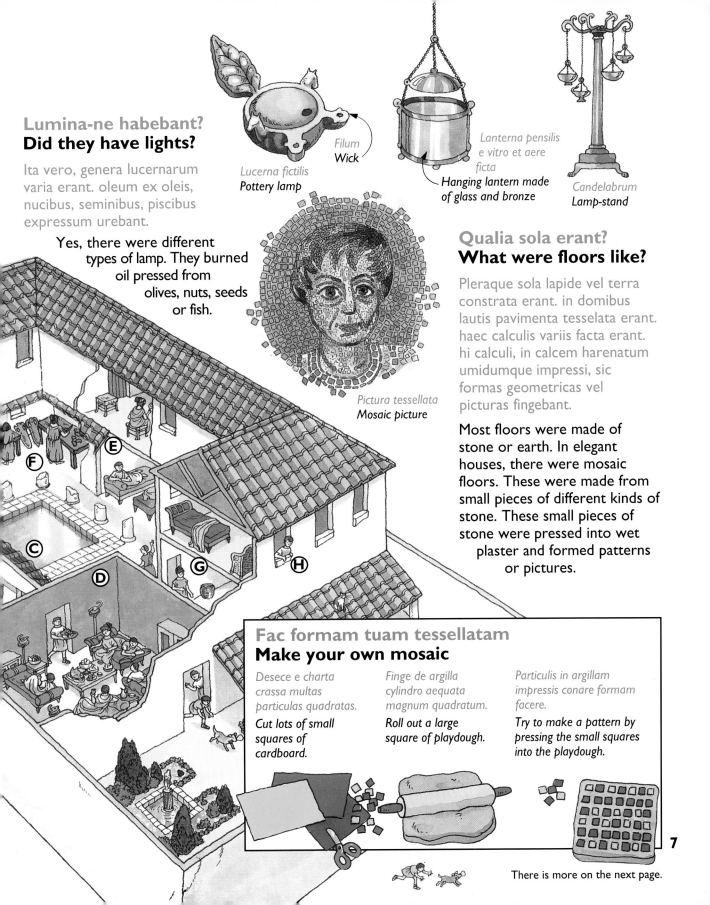

Fac formam tuam tessellatam
Make your own mosaic

Desece e charta crassa multas particulas quadratas.

Cut lots of small squares of cardboard.

Finge de argilla cylindro aequata magnum quadratum.

Roll out a large square of playdough.

Particulis in argillam impressis conare formam facere.

Try to make a pattern by pressing the small squares into the playdough.

7

There is more on the next page.

Quam supellectilem habebant?
What furniture did they have?

Supellectilem variam habebant. non solum e ligno vel vimine facta est, sed etiam e marmore vel aere. nonnulla supellex etiamnunc superest, nulla tamen supellex lignea aut viminea. haec omnis tabe consumpta est.

The Romans had all sorts of furniture. It was made of marble or metal, as well as wood or wicker. Some of the furniture has survived, though no wooden or wicker furniture. This has all rotted away.

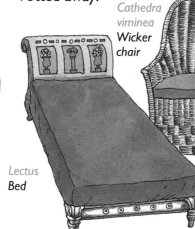

Cathedra viminea
Wicker chair

Mensa aere lignoque facta
Bronze and wood table

Scamnum
Stool

Lectus
Bed

Culinas-ne habebant?   # Did they have kitchens?

Culinae erant in domibus, nullae in cenaculis. eis qui in cenaculis habitabant necesse erat coctum emere.

There were kitchens in private houses, but none in apartments. People living in apartments had to buy ready-cooked food.

Veru
Spit

In domibus erant magnae culinae, huic similes.
Private houses had large
8 kitchens like this one.

Servus ansam versabat.
A slave turned the handle.

Incendium quo cibus in ollis coquebatur
Fire for cooking food in pots

Quomodo domos calefaciebant?
How did they heat their homes?

Excogitaverunt modum quo aer calidum sub suspensuras agebatur.

They invented a system for driving hot air under the floors.

Suspensura
Floor

Aer calidum
Hot air

Hypocausis
Furnace

Pilae **Pillars**

Fortasse calorem ex hypocause dilatum et moderari poterant: nemo scit.

Perhaps they could even control the heat from the furnace: nobody really knows.

Infra vides modum alium quo aer calidum differebatur.

Below you can see another hot-air system.

Suspensura
Floor

Tubae quae aer calidum ex hypocause ferebant
Pipes carrying hot air from the furnace

Fortasse nonnullis tubis obstructis calorem retinere poterant.
Perhaps they could keep the heat down by blocking off some of the pipes.

Ubi obsonabant? **Where did they go shopping?**

Multae tabernae in magnis oppidis erant.
pleraeque parvae erant, et in viam patebant.
a fronte stabat mensa; ei qui obsonabant in
via manebant.

There were lots of places to shop in large towns.
Most were small and opened onto the street.
There was a counter across the front, and
shoppers stayed in the street.

Hae tabernae sub cenaculis sunt.
These stalls are below apartments.

Titulus
Menu

Popina
Snack bar

Hi jus edunt.
These people are eating soup.

Domina cum servo qui cibaria fert
Mistress with her slave, who is
carrying the shopping

Qui obsonabant? **Who went shopping?**

Divites raro ad tabernas ipsi
ibant, nisi res privatas vel
sumptuosas sibi emere
volebant. cum alia, velut
cibum, requirebant, servos
mittebant.

Wealthy people rarely went
shopping themselves, except
when they wanted to buy
themselves personal or
expensive things. When they
wanted other things like food,
they sent their slaves.

Ubi in oppido cenabant? **Where did they eat out?**

Multae popinae et cauponae
erant. cibum potionemque
aut ibi consumere poterant
aut auferre.

There were plenty of snack
bars and wine bars. People
could have food and drink there
or they could take it away.

9

There is more on the next page.

Pharmacopolae erant?
Did they have pharmacists?

Pharmacopolae vero erant in oppidis Romanis. non solum medicamenta sed etiam carmina magica vendebant.

Yes, there were pharmacists in Roman towns. They sold magic spells as well as medicines.

Tabernarius cupas vini ad marcellum fert.
A stallholder brings his casks of wine to market.

Mercatus foris erant?
Did they have outdoor markets?

Certe omnia oppida nundinas habebant. tabernas in foro statuebant.

Yes, every town had regular market days. People set up market stalls in the town square.

Mercatus Romanus
A Roman market

Canis Romanus
Roman dog

Viae-ne unquam vehiculis obstructae sunt?
Were there ever traffic jams?

Ita vero, plaustra, quae res ad omnes mercatus ferebant, saepe vias in urbe Roma impediebant. qua de causa Julius Caesar plaustra currusque interdiu ab urbe prohibuit.

Yes, wagons trying to deliver goods to all the stores and stalls often blocked the streets in the city of Rome. Because of this, Julius Caesar banned wagons and chariots from the city during the day.

Laniena
A butcher's stall

Fur
A thief

Cetarius
A fishmonger

Pisces
Fish

Quomodo togas purgabant? How did people clean togas?

Fullones primum togas candidas nitro faciebant.

Toga-cleaners first bleached the togas with saltpetre.

Tum in creta fullonia cum aqua mixta lavabant.

Then they washed them in fuller's earth* mixed with water.

Deinde siccabant, complicabant, denique prelo premebant.

Once the togas had dried, they folded them and put them in a press.

*This is a special kind of clay.

Vela solem cibariis arcebant.
Awnings kept the sun off the food.

Pistrina
Baker's stall

Pomaria
Fruit stall

Praeco
Auctioneer

Servi
Slaves

Licentes
Bidders

Auctio servorum
A slave auction

Quid pro tegmine adhibebant?
What did they use as packaging?

Nihil. omnes suas amphoras, ollas, canistra secum afferebant.

Nothing. Everyone brought their own wine jars, pots and baskets along with them.

Servi res graves ferunt
Slaves carrying heavy shopping

Domina
Mistress

Ubi Romani servos emebant?
Where did Romans buy their slaves?

Servi saepe de terris a Romanis bello victis ducti erant. tum venalicii eos in foro exhibebant et vendebant ei qui maximum in auctione detulit.

Slaves were often people brought from countries that the Romans had conquered. Slave dealers put the slaves on show in the market square, and sold them by auction to the person who offered to pay the most.

Quae pecunia eis erat? # What was their money like?

Nummis utebantur aere, argento, auro fictis. nummi Romani multorum generum inventi sunt.

They used coins made of bronze, silver or gold. Many different kinds of Roman coin have been found.

Primus nummus Romanus, ex aere Cyprio signatus

The first Roman coin, minted out of copper

Primus nummus rotundus
The first round coin

Nummus argenteus, circiter anno CC a.Chr.n. signatus**

Silver coin, first minted around 200BC

Nummus qui mortem Julii Caesaris memorat
Coin that records the death of Julius Caesar

**CC is Latin for 200; also see footnote page 3.

Pueri Romani in ludum ibant?
Did Roman children go to school?

Tempore superiore filii divitiorum domi a magistris suis docebantur. postea magistri ludos puerorum constituerunt et mercedem poscebant. nec puellae nec pueri pauperes in ludum ibant.

In the early days, wealthier people's sons were taught at home by their own tutors. Later, teachers set up boys' schools and charged money. Girls and poor boys did not go to school.

Quanti erant ludi?
How big were the schools?

Pauci ludi amplius duodecim pueros recipiebant.

Few schools took more than twelve boys.

Hic magister Graecus est. multi magistri e Graecia venerunt.
This teacher is Greek. Many teachers came from Greece.

Puer neglegens
A boy not paying attention

Volumen
A scroll

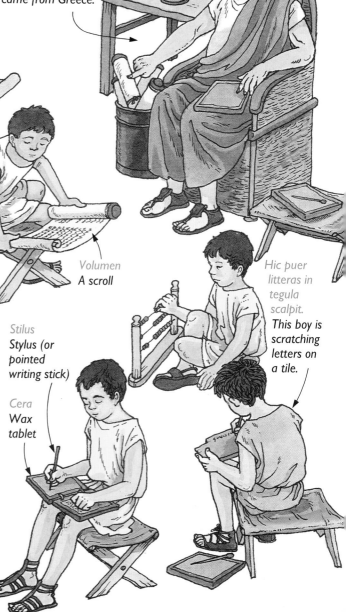

Stilus
Stylus (or pointed writing stick)

Cera
Wax tablet

Hic puer litteras in tegula scalpit.
This boy is scratching letters on a tile.

In quo scribebant?
What did they write on?

Romani scribebant in charta, papyro facta, et in membranis. Haec pretiosissima erant, itaque discipuli plerumque ceris et stilo utebantur. ceris identidem uti poterant.

The Romans wrote on paper made from papyrus reeds, and also on parchment.* These were very expensive, so pupils mostly used wax tablets and a pointed writing stick. They could keep on reusing the tablets.

12

*Papyrus is a kind of reed; parchment was made from animal skins.

Libros-ne legebant?
Did they read books?

Libri pretiosissimi erant. arte impressoria nondum inventa, libri Romanorum manu scribebantur. primo libri formam voluminis habebant (charta in umbilicos convoluta). postea codex inventus est. quamquam formam libri hodierni habebat, etiamtum manu scribebatur.

Books were very expensive. As printing had not yet been invented, Roman books were written by hand. At first books were scrolls (paper rolled around sticks). Later the codex was invented, which was still hand-written but shaped like a modern book.

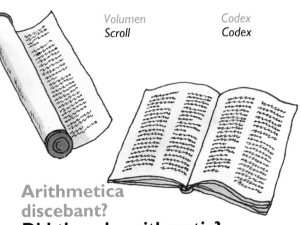

Volumen
Scroll

Codex
Codex

Arithmetica discebant?
Did they do arithmetic?

Profecto, sed numeri Romani alii ac nostri erant. numeros ab uno ad duodecim infra videre potes.

Of course, but Roman numbers were different from ours. You can see numbers one to twelve below.

Abacus: hoc utebantur cum numerabant.
An abacus: they used this for counting.

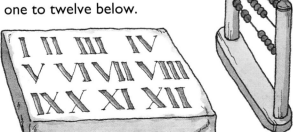

Quibus artibus aliis studebant?
What other subjects did they study?

Pueri non solum legere, scribere, numerare, sed etiam Graece loqui discebant. si iuvenes aut rei publicae aut iuri incumbere volebant, multos annos arti dicendi studere necesse erat.

As well as reading, writing and counting, boys learned to speak Greek. Older boys who wanted to be politicians or lawyers had to study speaking in public for many years.

Rhetor
Public speaking teacher

Ecquid puellae discebant?
Did girls learn anything?

Filiae divitiorum et legere et scribere et res domesticas curare discebant. multae etiam musica docebantur.

Wealthier people's daughters learned to read and write, and also how to run a household. Many had music lessons too.

Lyra
Lyre

Doctor musicorum Music teacher

Nos numeris Romanis utimur?
Do we use Roman numbers?

Ita vero, etiamnunc ad res quasdam numeris Romanis utimur. ecquae in mentem veniunt?

Yes. Roman numbers are still used today for some things. Are there any you can think of?

Quid aegri faciebant?
What did they do if they were ill?

Nonnulli Romano morbo affecti in fanis Aesculapii, dei medicinae, incubebant. ibi in somniis, ut credebant, remedia cognoverunt. plerique tamen medicos visebant.

When they were ill, some Romans slept in shrines to the god of medicine, Aesculapius. They thought the dreams they had there told them how to get better. Most people, however, went to see the doctor.

Quid de medicis Romanis cognovimus?
What do we know about Roman doctors?

Divitissimi medicos suos habebant. pauperes aegri gratis a medicis curabantur qui vectigalia pensitare non debebant.

Very rich people had their own doctors. Poor people who were sick were treated free by doctors who did not have to pay any taxes.

Medici in valetudinariis vel in medicorum scholis disciplinam accipiebant. omnes fere medici viri erant.

Doctors got their training in army hospitals or medical schools. Nearly all doctors were men.

Nonnullae autem medicae erant. hae, ut plerique hodie credunt, gravidas curabant.

There were some women doctors too. Today most people think that these women doctors looked after pregnant women.

In hoc lapide medica sculpta est.
A woman doctor is shown on this carved stone.

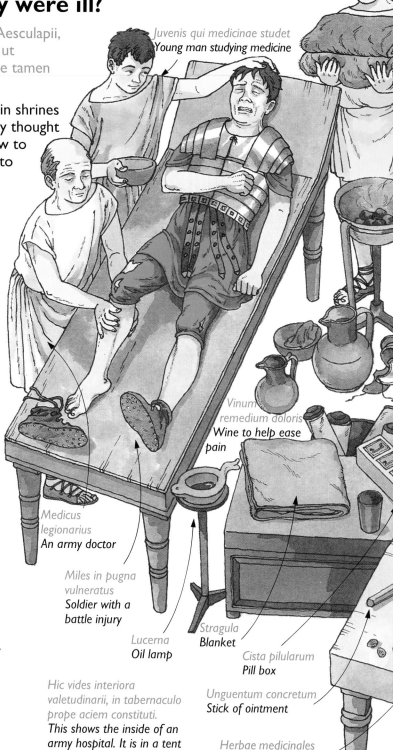

Juvenis qui medicinae studet
Young man studying medicine

Medicus legionarius
An army doctor

Miles in pugna vulneratus
Soldier with a battle injury

Lucerna
Oil lamp

Vinum remedium doloris
Wine to help ease pain

Stragula
Blanket

Cista pilularum
Pill box

Unguentum concretum
Stick of ointment

Herbae medicinales
Herbs for medicine

Hic vides interiora valetudinarii, in tabernaculo prope aciem constituti.
This shows the inside of an army hospital. It is in a tent near the battlefield.

FIL·MEDICA

Corpora-ne secabant?
Did they perform operations?

Medici Romani multos casus gravissimos curabant. viscera secare, ossa fracta restituere, membra excidere poterant.

Roman doctors took care of many very serious medical conditions. They could operate on internal organs, mend broken bones and cut off limbs.

Multi feliciter secti sunt. difficilius erat vitam aegrorum postea conservare. nulla enim medicamenta erant quae contagionem prohibere poterant.

Many people had successful operations. What was harder was making sure the patients lived afterwards. There were no good drugs to stop infection.

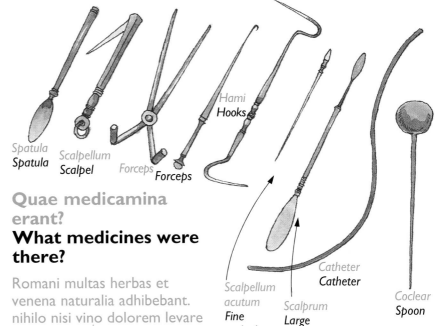

Spatula — *Spatula*
Scalpellum — *Scalpel*
Forceps — *Forceps*
Hami — *Hooks*
Scalpellum acutum — *Fine scalpel*
Scalprum — *Large scalpel*
Catheter — *Catheter*
Coclear — *Spoon*

Instrumenta Romanorum chirurgica
Roman surgical instruments

Quae medicamina erant?
What medicines were there?

Romani multas herbas et venena naturalia adhibebant. nihilo nisi vino dolorem levare poterant, non omnino comprimere.

The Romans used lots of herbs and natural drugs. The only thing they had to relieve pain was wine, but that could not stop it completely.

Quid de ossibus reperimus?
What do bones tell us?

Foramina a medico sollertissimo terebrata
Holes made by a very skilled doctor

Reliquiis in sepulcris detectis sollertiam medicorum Romanorum intelligimus.

The remains found in tombs tell us about the skills of Roman doctors.

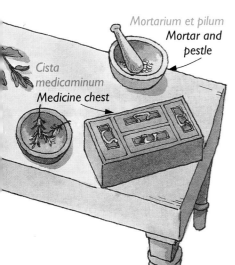

Cista medicaminum
Medicine chest

Mortarium et pilum
Mortar and pestle

Dentes falsos habebant?
Did they have false teeth?

Ita vero, pauci saltem divites. dentes falsi fingebantur de ebore et auro, quod numquam robigine laeditur.

Yes, or at least a few wealthy people did. False teeth were made of ivory and gold, which never rusts.

Hi dentes falsi tanti depicti sunt quanti veri similes sunt.
These false teeth are shown at their actual size.

MILLFIELD PREP SCHOOL
LIBRARY

Quomodo Romani se oblectabant?
What did the Romans do for fun?

Romani multis ludis fruebantur. aut domi ludebant aut ad theatrum adibant. ingentia spectacula etiam frequentare amabant, velut ludos circenses vel gladiatorios.

The Romans had lots of pastimes. They played games at home or went to the theatre. They also loved going to huge public sports events like chariot races and gladiator fights.

Quos ludos pueri ludebant?
What games did children play?

Erant pueris petaura, aeorae, aieti, trochi et casae quibus ludebant. et pupae erant, sed nulli ursilli.

Children had seesaws, swings, kites, hoops and toy houses to play with. There were dolls too, but no teddy bears.

Et pueri et adulti talis ludere amabant.

Both children and grown-ups loved playing knucklebones.

Tabula lusoria et calculi
A game board and pieces

Tali eodem modo ac tessera jaciebantur.
Knucklebones were used like dice.

Pupa cum bracchiis cruribusque articulatis
Doll with joints in its arms and legs

Quae erant curricula?
What were chariot races?

Ex omnibus ludis hos Romani maxime amabant. aliquando uno die viginti quattuor curricula erant.

They were the sports the Romans loved most of all. Sometimes there were twenty-four races a day.

Currus erat carrus parvus duarum rotarum equis velocibus tractus. hoc everso, auriga saepissime occisus est.

A chariot was a small two-wheeled cart pulled by fast horses. If it tipped over, the driver was usually killed.

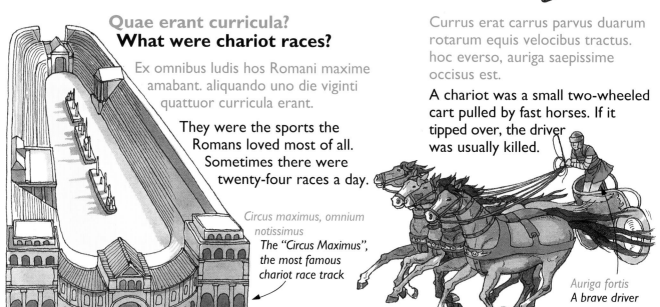

Circus maximus, omnium notissimus
The "Circus Maximus", the most famous chariot race track

Auriga fortis
A brave driver

Quae erant munera? **What were gladiator fights?**

Erant ludi quos plebs amabat. gladiatores plurimis spectantibus non solum inter se sed etiam cum bestiis pugnare cogebantur.

They were very popular shows. Fighters called gladiators were made to fight wild animals, as well as each other, in front of big crowds.

Cassis
Helmet

Parma
Small round shield

Threx
A "Thracian"

Samnis
A "Samnite"

Pugio
Dagger

Rete
Net

Ocrea
Leg covering

Murmillo, gladiator optime protectus
A "Murmillo", the best protected gladiator

Hic vides gladiatores quattuor generum et nomina Latina. armis et vestitu inter se differebant.
Here you can see four types of gladiator, and their Latin names. They had different equipment and clothing.

Tridens
Trident

Retiarius
A "Retiarius"

Qui erant gladiatores?
Who were gladiators?

Erant servi, scelesti, captivi. pugnare cogebantur. si vicerunt aliquando libertatem adepti sunt.

They were slaves, criminals or prisoners of war. They were forced to fight. If they won, they were sometimes set free.

Quid pollex sublatus significabat?

Ad finem certaminis imperator pollice sublato vel verso vitam vel mortem victo indicabat. pollex sublatus, ut plerique putant, vitam significabat.

Imperator
The emperor

Pollex imperatoris
The emperor's thumb

What did thumbs up mean?

At the end of a fight, the emperor gave a thumbs up or thumbs down signal, which meant he wanted the loser to live or die. Most people think that thumbs up meant "live".

17

There is more on the next page.

Ubi fabulae dabantur?
Where were plays put on?

In theatris, quae primum e materie nullis cum sedilibus aedificabantur. postea multo maiores e lapide cum sedilibus lapideis aedificabantur.

In theatres, which at first were built of wood and had no seats. Later they were much bigger and were built of stone, with stone seats.

Quae erant fabulae Romanae?
What were Roman plays like?

Aut comoediae aut tragoediae erant. finis comoediae semper felix erat, finis tragoediae tristis vel luctuosa.

They were either comedies or tragedies. A comedy always had a happy ending, a tragedy had a sad or gloomy one.

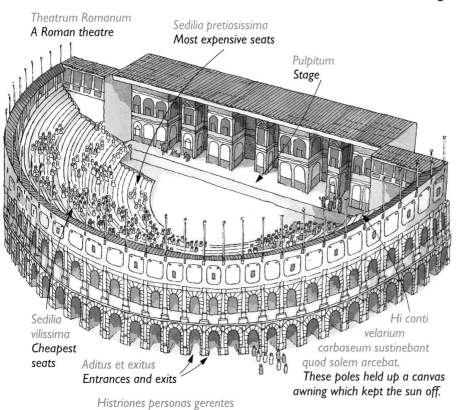

Theatrum Romanum
A Roman theatre

Sedilia pretiosissima
Most expensive seats

Pulpitum
Stage

Sedilia vilissima
Cheapest seats

Aditus et exitus
Entrances and exits

Hi conti velarium carbaseum sustinebant quod solem arcebat.
These poles held up a canvas awning which kept the sun off.

Histriones personas gerentes
Actors wearing masks

Quid scimus de histrionibus Romanis?
What do we know about Roman actors?

Omnes histriones viri erant. feminae quas in pictura supra vides viri sunt qui vestes femineas induerunt.

All actors were men. The women you can see in the picture above are men dressed up as women.

Cur histriones saepe personas induerunt?
Why did actors often wear masks?

Dramatis personae in multis fabulis eaedem erant, velut "stultus ridens" vel "senex sapiens". itaque personae has partes procul spectantibus melius patefaciebant.

Many plays had the same characters in them, like "the smiling fool" or "the wise old man". Masks were a good way of making these parts clear to an audience that was far away.

18

Romani convivia agitabant?
Did the Romans have parties?

Certe convivia amabant. multi dies festi, multae feriae erant cum saepe convivia apparabant. divites hospitibus vina et epulas conquisitas dabant.

Yes, they loved parties. There were many festivals and public holidays, and they often had parties then. Wealthy people treated their guests to wonderful wines and food.

Puer vinum fundit.
A slave pours wine.

Servi
Slaves

Dominus
Their master

Saturnalibus domini servis serviebant.
At the Saturnalia (the god Saturn's festival), masters waited on their slaves.

Convivium
A party

Lectus
Couch

Lyra
Lyre

Epulis musici convivas oblectant.
During the feast, musicians entertain the guests.

Quem cibum epulantes edebant?
What food did they eat at feasts?

Gustationem acetaria, ova, conchas edebant, deinde cenam ad septem fercula - carnem, olera, liquamina multarum generum.

They ate salads, eggs and shellfish as a first course, followed by a main course of up to seven dishes. These were meat dishes, vegetables and sauces.

Tuba
A Roman trumpet

Tibiae
Double pipes

Lyra ligno aereque ficta
A lyre made of wood and metal

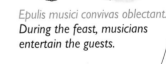

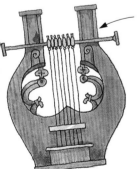

Sistrum
A sistrum (a rattle-like instrument)

Musicam amabant?
Did they like music?

Ita vero, musica saepe se delectabant. multa et varia instrumenta musica eis erant.

Yes, they often entertained themselves with music. They had lots of different musical instruments.

19

Piscinae erant? Did they have swimming pools?

Multa balnea privata et publica erant. thermae etiam erant, aedificia magnifica qua non solum in piscina natare sed etiam se exercere, lavare, in laconico laxare, iatralipti committere solebant.

There were lots of small public and private bathhouses. There were also big bathhouses, wonderful places where they would not only swim in a swimming pool, but also exercise, wash, relax in a steam bath and have a massage.

Qui in balnea ibant?
Who went to the baths?

Viri feminae pueri thermis utebantur, sed separatim. feminae plerumque vesperi adibant.

Men, women and children used the baths, but not together. Women usually went in the evenings.

Thermae
A Roman bathhouse

Gratis intrare licebat?
Could you go in free?

Non licebat, sed pretium erat minimum. Romani munditiam magni aestimabant.

No, but the entrance fee was very low. The Romans felt that keeping clean was really important.

Laconicum
Hot steam bath

Sudans
A sweaty man

Iatraliptes
Masseur

Qualia erant balnea? What were bathhouses like?

Mirabilia! aqua balnearum ita calefiebat ut aliud calidum esset, alium tepidum, alium frigidum, et ex alio ad aliud errabant. thermae saepe magnifice exornatae sunt.

Wonderful! The water in the baths was heated so that there was a hot pool, a warm pool and a cool one, and you could wander from one to the other. Big bathhouses were often beautifully decorated.

Apodyterium
Changing room

Ubi natabant? **Where did they go swimming?**

Non intra aedificia balnearum (lacus enim minores erant) sed in piscinis veris, quae sub divo erant.

Not inside the bathhouse buildings (the pools were too small) but in real swimming pools, which were out in the open air.

Cenacula ad strepitum obnoxia
Apartments, which would have been very noisy

Hi luctantur.
These men are wrestling.

Piscina
Swimming pool

Quomodo se lavabant? **How did they wash?**

Corpora oleo pro sapone fricabant, quod strigile destringebant.

They rubbed their bodies with olive oil, not soap, and scraped it off with a scraper.

Lagena
Oil flask

Nonnullorum servi corpora destringebant.

Some people had their slaves do the scraping for them.

Tres strigiles in circulo tentae. aere, ossibis, ligno fingebantur.
Three scrapers kept on a ring. Scrapers were made of metal, bone or wood.

Animalia Romani alebant?
Did the Romans keep animals?

Romani animalia colligebant, animi causa alebant, etiam venabantur. animalia quaedam mansuefaciebant quae carrus traherent aut res et homines ferrent.

The Romans collected animals, kept them as pets and even hunted them. They tamed some animals so they would pull carts and carry goods and people.

Venatio aprum
Wild boar hunt

Haec tabula abhinc amplius duo milia annorum facta est. verba "cave canem" nos etiamnunc videmus.
This picture is over 2000 years old. We can still see the words "Beware of the dog" on it.

Cur Romani venabantur?
Why did the Romans go hunting?

Alimentorum causa venari et piscari solebant. etiam feras vivas laqueis captabant ut ad ludos mitterent.

They hunted and fished for food. They also trapped live wild animals to send them to the shows.

Romani saepta ferarum habebant?
Did the Romans have zoos?

Immo feras inusitatas captas multitudini exhibebant. animalia vulgaria, velut tauros vel ursos, cum gladiatoribus pugnare cogebant.

No, but when they caught unusual wild animals, they showed them to the crowds. They made common animals like bulls and bears fight gladiators.

Animalia ex Romam ad missa sunt.
Animals were sent from Africa to Rome for the public shows.

Africa ludos

Hic elephas Africanus ludis interest.
This African elephant is taking part in a show.

Homines revera ad leones missi sunt?
Were people really thrown to the lions?

Homines ad leones interdum missi sunt. sic ludis scelesti, Christiani, Judaei a bestiis laniabantur.

Yes, people were sometimes thrown to the lions. Criminals, Christians and Jews were torn to pieces by wild beasts at the shows.

Quae animalia in fundis alebant? What farm animals did they keep?

Animalia omnis generis alimenti causa alebant: gallinas, columbas, sues, capras, oves et cetera. caseum e lacte caprarum ovumque presso factum amabant. multa animalia ad laborem servabant.

They kept all kinds of animals for food: chickens, pigeons, pigs, goats, sheep and so on. They loved cheese made from goat and sheep's milk. They also kept lots of working animals.

Canis
Dog

Anseres
Geese

Sues
Pigs

Petasus
A sun hat

Alvi
Beehives

Agricola infelix
An unlucky farmer

Hic capram mulget.
This man is milking a goat.

Oves
Sheep

Caprae
Goats

Boves laborantes
Working oxen

Frumentum
Corn

Asinus circumambulans frumentum inter molas molit.
The donkey grinds the corn between the millstones by walking around in a circle.

Quae animalia ad laborem servabant?
What working animals did they keep?

Boves, mulos, asinos exercebant ut plaustra traherent, farinam molerent, onera gravia transportarent.

They kept working oxen, mules and donkeys to pull carts, grind corn, and carry heavy loads.

Frumentum saepe hoc modo in pistrina molebatur.
Flour was often ground like this in a bakery.

Filius pistoris
Baker's son

Frumentum molitum, vel farina
Ground corn, or flour

Hoc sciebas?
Did you know?

Imperator Caligula mente alienatus est. equum consulem creare conatus est. consulatus erat honor amplissimus!

The emperor Caligula went mad. He tried to make his horse consul. This was the top job in the government!

Caligula
Caligula

Senator sollicitus
A worried senator

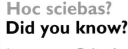

Equus Caligulae praetextatus
Caligula's horse, wearing a top official's toga

23

Fidem Deo habebant? Did they believe in God?

Per omne fere imperii tempus, Romani multis deis deabusque fidem habebant. munere suo quisque deus fungebatur.

During most of the time of the Empire, the Romans believed in many gods and goddesses. Each one had his or her own special duty.

Unde venerunt dei Romani?
Where did the Roman gods come from?

Multi dei Romanorum primum a Graecis culti erant. Romani eis nomina Romana dederunt.

Many of the Romans' gods had first been worshipped by the Greeks. The Romans gave them Roman names.

Lararium in domo
A household altar in a Roman home

Hic pater, mater, filius Lares orant.
Here a father, mother and their son are praying to the household spirits.

Qui erant Lares?
Who were the Lares?

Omnes domus suis geniis defendebantur, qui "Lares" vocabantur.

Every house was watched over by its own spirits, who were **24** called "Lares".

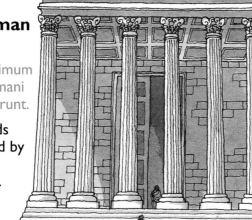

Templum Romanum Graeco simile
A Roman temple, similar to a Greek one

Quae erant templa?
What were temples?

Templum erat domicilium terrestre unius dei vel deae. sacerdotes sacra templi curabant.

A temple was the earthly home of a particular god or goddess. Priests and priestesses looked after the temple's sacred objects.

Credebant vitam post mortem esse?
Did they believe in an afterlife?

Anima mortui, ut Romani credebant, cumba trans Stygium flumen ad inferos vehebatur.

The Romans believed that a dead person's soul was taken by boat across the River Styx to the underworld.

Styx flumen inferos circumvenit.
The River Styx surrounded the underworld.

Aditus inferorum, quem Cerberus canis triceps custodiebat.
The entrance to the underworld was guarded by Cerberus, a three-headed dog.

Anima mortui a judice inferorum ad Elysium vel Tartara missa est.

The dead person's soul was sent to heaven or hell by the judge of the underworld.

Jupiter deus forma tauri se dissimulans
The god Jupiter disguised as a bull

Cur tot dei erant? Why were there so many gods?

Provinciam suam quisque deus curabat, velut Ceres, quae dea agri culturae erat. ideo agricolae eam orabant. dei maiores hic et in pagina proxima describuntur. nomina Graeca in uncis indicantur.

Each god looked after his or her own area of life. For instance, Ceres was goddess of agriculture, so farmers prayed to her. The more important gods are shown here and on the next page. Their Greek names are shown in brackets.

Jupiter (Zeus) deorum rex, fulminum jaculator
Jupiter (Zeus), king of the gods, hurler of thunderbolts

Juno (Hera), feminarum et partus dea
Juno (Hera), goddess of women and childbirth

Mercurius (Hermes), Jovis nuntius, negotiorum et furum deus
Mercury (Hermes), Jupiter's messenger and god of trade and thieves

Minerva (Athena), sapientiae et artium dea
Minerva (Athena), goddess of wisdom and crafts

Bacchus (Dionysus), vini deus
Bacchus (Dionysus), god of wine

Quae erant Virgines Vestales?

Vesta dea templum suum habebat. incendium perpetuo intra ardebat. "flamma extincta ruet imperium!" inquiebant Romani. feminae sex, Virgines Vestales vocatae, incendium curabant. annos triginta hoc faciebant; hoc tempore matrimonio prohibitae sunt.

Virgines Vestales
The Vestal Virgins

Who were the Vestal Virgins?

The goddess Vesta had her own temple. Inside was a fire that burned non-stop. "If the flame goes out, the empire will collapse!" said the Romans. Six women, called the Vestal Virgins, looked after it. They did this for thirty years and could not marry in that time.

25

There is more about religion on the next two pages.

Quae dei agebant? **What did the gods do?**

Dei numina sibi propria habebant, sed etiam idem ac homines se gerebant. inter se rixabantur, invidebant, et fallere conabantur.

The gods had their own special powers, but they also behaved like human beings. They argued, got jealous, and even tried to trick each other.

Sacerdotes taurum Marti belli deo mactaturi
Priests about to sacrifice a bull to Mars, god of war

Diana (Artemis), venationis et lunae dea
Diana (Artemis), goddess of hunting and the moon

Neptunus (Poseidon), maris deus
Neptune (Poseidon), god of the sea

Venus (Aphrodite), amoris et pulchritudinis dea
Venus (Aphrodite), goddess of love and beauty

Animalia Romani mactabant? **Did the Romans sacrifice animals?**

Saepe animalia Romani deis mactabant. haruspices et exta inspiciebant ut futura praedicerent.

The Romans often sacrificed animals to the gods. Special priests also examined their guts to tell the future.

Elige deos **Spot the gods**

Si caelamina, signa, picturas deorum Romanorum diligenter inspicies, cernere qui sint poteris. qui sunt hi tres?

By examining carvings, statues and paintings of the Roman gods, you can tell who they all are. Who are these three? (See bottom of page 27 for answers.)

Caelamen
A carving

Signum marmoreum
A marble statue

Pictura in tabula
A wall-painting

Dea tristis et tempora anni The sad goddess and the seasons

A principio cum dei etiamtum terram ambulabant, Ceres frugum dea filiam pulcherrimam Proserpinam habebat. Dis, inferorum deus, amore Proserpinae captus est. quia Proserpina in inferis secum vivere nolebat (hoc Dis pro certo habebat), eam in curru surripuit.

Long ago, when the gods still walked the earth, Ceres, goddess of crops, had a beautiful daughter called Proserpina. Dis, god of the underworld, fell in love with Proserpina. Because she would not live with him in the underworld (Dis was sure of this), he kidnapped her in his chariot.

Ceres filiam terra marique quaesivit. omnia alia non flocci faciebat. mox fruges deficiebant, homines fame peribant. tum raptu Proserpinae cognita auxilium a Jove petivit.

Ceres searched for her daughter over land and sea. Nothing else mattered to her. Soon the crops began to fail and people were starving. Then she found out about Proserpina's kidnapping and asked Jupiter for his help.

Jupiter deorum rex, "Proserpinam tibi reddam," inquit, "si nullum inferorum cibum consumpserit." adhuc nihil gustaverat Proserpina, nam tristior erat, sed a Dite dolo decepta sex semina granati edit.

Jupiter, king of the gods, said, "I will give Proserpina back to you so long as she has not eaten any food of the dead in the underworld." Up to then, Proserpina had not eaten anything as she was too sad, but Dis tricked her into eating six pomegranate seeds.

Jupiter, propter hunc dolum ira incensus est. Proserpina ad matrem redire sivit, sed sex menses anni cuiusque cum Dite in inferis agere debuit quod sex semina ederat.

Jupiter was enraged by this trick. He allowed Proserpina to go back to her mother, but from then on she had to spend six months of each year with Dis in the underworld. Each month stood for one of the six pips she had eaten.

Omnibus annis filia liberata Ceres felix erat et fruges virebant. hoc tempus ver et aestas erat.

Every year when her daughter was released, Ceres was happy and the crops thrived. This was spring and summer.

Ubi tamen Proserpina ad inferos redivit, Ceres tristitia victa est: folia cadebant, nihil provenit. illud tempus auctumnus et hiems erat. sic tempora anni varia originem habuerunt.

When Proserpina returned to the underworld, Ceres became sad. The leaves started to fall and nothing grew. This was autumn and winter. This is how the different seasons came about.

Answer to "Spot the gods", from left to right: Minerva, Bacchus, Mercury.

Qui erat exercitus Romanus?
What was the Roman army like?

Ingentissimus erat et optime ordinatus. aliquando ad quadringenta quinquaginta milia militum erant.

It was very big and very well organized. At one time, there were as many as 450, 000 soldiers.

Qui erant milites?
Who were the soldiers?

Ubi Romanis erat urbs sola necdum imperium, cives in exercitum ad pauca stipendia interdum conscribebantur. ab anno C a.Chr.n plurimi milites sua sponte nomina dabant.

Before Rome had an empire, citizens were sometimes made to serve in the army for a few years. By 100BC, most soldiers were volunteers.

Exercitus in legiones divisus est. legioni erant cohortes X, cohorti centuriae VI, centuriae milites LXXX.

The army was divided into legions. A legion contained ten cohorts, a cohort contained six centuries, and a century 80 soldiers.

Milites legionarii
Foot soldiers

Centurio
A centurion, leader of a century

Tribunus militum
A military tribune, leader of a cohort

Legatus, dux legionis
A legate, commander of a legion

Qualia erant castra?
What was an army camp like?

In castris stativis erant aedificia materie vel lapide constructa, in castris aestivis tabernacula.

In a permanent camp, there were buildings made of timber or stone, but in a summer camp there were tents.

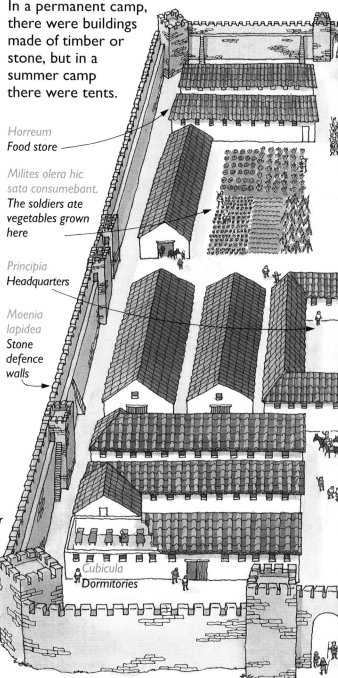

Horreum
Food store

Milites olera hic sata consumebant.
The soldiers ate vegetables grown here

Principia
Headquarters

Moenia lapidea
Stone defence walls

Cubicula
Dormitories

Multa equorum stabula erant.
The camp had lots of stables for the cavalry.

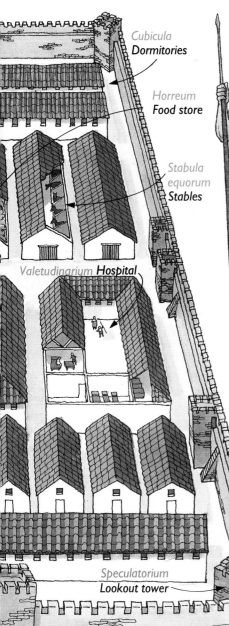

Cubicula
Dormitories

Horreum
Food store

Stabula equorum
Stables

Valetudinarium **Hospital**

Speculatorium
Lookout tower

Qui vestitus, quae arma eis erant?
What uniform and weapons did they have?

Alii milites alias vestes gerebant. multa genera armorum erant, a pugionibus ad acies.

Different soldiers wore different things. There were many types of weapons, from daggers to battering rams.

Lorica segmentata
Breast plate

Pila
Javelins

Pellis
Animal skin

Signum
Standard

Miles legionarius
Legionary

Signifer
Standard bearer

Signum suum quisque legio habebat. omnibus aquila erat.
Each legion had its own standard. These all had an eagle.

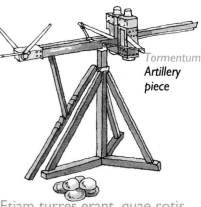

Tormentum
Artillery piece

Etiam turres erant, quae rotis promovebantur ut milites in moenia oppidi desilirent.

There were also siege towers. These were moved up on wheels so that the soldiers could jump down onto the walls of a town.

Quae erat testudo?
What was the tortoise?

Aliquando in pugna milites conglobati et scuta super capita tenentes tegmentum fecerunt quod "testudo" vocabatur.

In battle, soldiers sometimes grouped together holding up their shields like a protective shell. This was called the "tortoise".

Testudo
A Roman army tortoise

Quae alia Romani aedificabant?
What else did the Romans build?

Non solum templa, thermas, domus aedificabant, sed etiam aquae ductus, pontes, vias.

As well as temples, bathhouses and houses, the Romans built aqueducts, bridges and roads.

Hic aquae ductus et via ducuntur.
Here an aqueduct and a road are being built.

Qui erat aquae ductus?
What was an aqueduct?

Canalis erat qui aquam a fonte vel rivo in oppidum ferebat. alii aquae ductus subterranei erant, alii, pontibus similes aedificati, aquam per dorsum ferebant.

It was a channel that carried water from a spring or stream into a town. Some aqueducts were underground. Others were built like bridges and carried the water along the top.

Materies contignationis
Wood for building scaffolding

Quam sollers dispositio!
What a clever design!

Aquae ductus, pontibus similes, sollerte disponebantur. clivo minuto ducebantur ut aqua semper cursu recto flueret. multi super LVII pedes alti erant, unus XXXVI milia passuum longa.

The bridge-like aqueducts were cleverly designed. They were built at a slight slope so the water would always flow the right way. Many were over 57 Roman feet high and **30** one was 36 Roman miles long.*

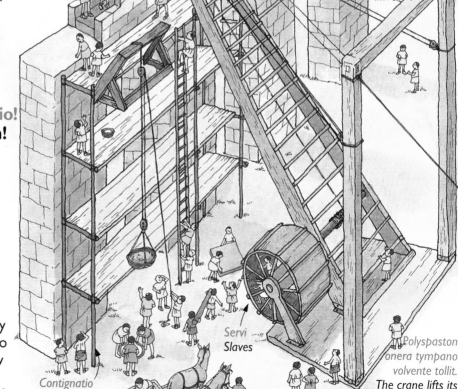

Contignatio
Wooden scaffolding

Servi
Slaves

Polyspaston onera tympano volvente tollit.
The crane lifts its load when the treadmill turns.

*See page 32.

Via
Road

Servi laborantes
Slaves hard at
work

Milites viam novam
munientes
Soldiers building the new
road

Muli fessi
Tired mules

Cur viae Romanae adeo notae sunt?
Why are Roman roads so famous?

Quia tam firme munitae, tam rectae erant.
nostrae viae idem iter ac Romanae saepe
sequuntur. ad viam novam iter brevissimum et
aequissimum electum est. terra effossa lapides varia
magnitudine in fossam immissi sunt. summum
corium curvatum est ut aqua pluvia deflueret.

Because they were so well made and so straight.
Many modern roads follow the same route as
Roman ones. For a new road, the shortest and
flattest route was chosen. A trench was dug and
different sized stones were put in it. The top
layer was curved so rainwater would drain off.

Exemplum viae
Romanae
A typical Roman road

Media via curvata
The curved middle
of the road

Fossa aquae
pluviae
Ditch for rainwater

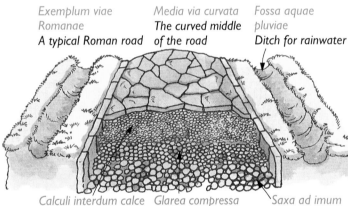

Calculi interdum calce
harenata mixtum
Small stones,
sometimes mixed
with cement

Glarea compressa
Tightly-packed
gravel

Saxa ad imum
strata
Bottom layer of
large stones

Alti et tuti   High and safe

Aquae ductus alti tutiores erant quod nemo
aquam subducere aut venenum inicere poterat.

High aqueducts were safer because nobody
could steal the water or put poison in it.

Quo aqua ibat?   Where did the water go?

Cum aqua ex aquae ductu in urbem advenisset
per tubulas plumbeas subterraneas emissa est.
ad bibendum, lavandum, multa alia adhibebatur.

When water from an aqueduct reached a city,
it was distributed through underground lead
pipes. It was used for drinking and washing
and lots else.

Rota aquaria
A water wheel

Aqua rotam
circumagit.
Water turns the
wheel.

Rota molas
circumagit.
The wheel turns the
millstones.

Molea
frumentum
molunt.
Stones
grind the
corn.

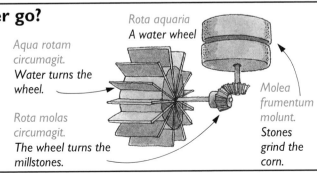

31

Latin notes

On this page you can find help with the most difficult Latin expressions used in this book, and with words whose meaning may not be obvious.

When printing Latin nowadays, capital letters are used at the start of paragraphs and names, but not at the start of each sentence. The book follows this custom.

Page 2

amplius	more than
quo tempore	at the time when
caput	head; on this page, it is used to mean "person"
proprium	property

Page 3

ei erant inimici   here, esse (to be) is used with the dative case to mean "to have"

Page 4

licebat	it was allowed; this is an impersonal verb
species	appearance
uti	to use; uti is followed by

the ablative case; it is a deponent verb (a passive verb with an active meaning)

Page 5

facies	face
faex	wine lees, dregs
adhibere	to use, to apply (to)

Page 6

pictura	painting, picture
tabula	tablet on which a picture is painted, picture

Page 7

calculus	small piece of stone
lumina-ne	the ending ne is

sometimes added to the first word of a sentence to show that it is a question

cylindro aequare   to flatten with a roller

Page 8

necesse esse	to be necessary for (followed by the dative case)
differre, dilatum	to spread around

Page 9

cibaria   foodstuffs

Page 10

candidus	white
prelum	press

Page 11

tegmen	covering, wrapping
ducere	to lead, to bring

Page 12

cera	wax, piece of wood covered with wax
stilus	stylus (writing stick, sharp

at one end for writing with, flat at the other end for rubbing the wax smooth)

Page 14

remedium	remedy, cure
gratis	free (adverb)
concretum	solidified

Page 15

secare	to cut
nihilo nisi	by nothing except
laedere	to hurt, to damage
terebrare	to bore (drill)
detegere	to uncover

Page 16

oblectare	to entertain
frui	to enjoy (deponent verb, followed by the ablative case)

ludi circenses   shows or games which took place in a "circus" (a race track)

jacere   to throw

Page 17

adipisci   to get (a deponent verb: passive with active meaning)

Page 18

persona   character, mask

Page 19

epulari   to feast (deponent verb: passive with active meaning)

Page 20

magni aestimare   to value highly

Page 22

animi causa	for the sake of pleasure
alere	to feed, to nurture
qui-dam	some, certain (only the first part, qui, changes case)
trahere	to pull (traherent, the subjunctive, is used to indicate purpose)
solere	to be accustomed to (followed by an infinitive)
laqueus	snare, trap
ut	this means "in order to"

when it is used with a subjunctive verb

Page 23

fundus	farm
sevare	to keep

Page 24

fidem habere	to have faith in (followed by the dative case)
fungi	to perform (deponent verb, followed by the ablative case)
inferi	inhabitants of the underworld
quis-que	each (only quis changes case)

Page 25

provincia	sphere of influence (of an official)
ideo	for that reason

Page 27

a principio	in the beginning
non flocci facere	not to care a straw for

Page 28

stipendium mereri   to earn a year's pay, to serve (for a year)

Page 30

ducere	to lead, to build (a road or wall)
pes	foot; a Roman foot = 296mm (11¾in)
mille passus	1000 paces, or

one Roman mile = 1.36 km (nearly a mile); a passus was a left and right step

Page 31

ad bibendum   for drinking (gerund of the verb bibere, to drink)

This bilingual edition first published in 1995 by Usborne Publishing Ltd, Usborne House, 83-85 Saffron Hill, London ECIN 8RT. Based on a previous title first published in 1993.
Copyright © 1995, 1993, Usborne Publishing Ltd.
Printed in Belgium.
The name Usborne and the device 🎈 are Trade Marks of Usborne Publishing Ltd.
All rights reserved. No part of this publication may be reproduced, stored in a retrieval system or transmitted in any form or by any means, electronic, mechanical, photocopying, recording or otherwise, without the prior permission of the publisher. UE

A.N. 08937	D. 870
DATE NOV 2000		7.99